TEWKESBURY ABBEY

Left:
Lord Gage, MP for the Borough of Tewkesbury, presented these fine wrought-iron gates to the abbey in 1734. The workmanship is attributed to William Edney.

Contents

Right: ⑤
The superb lierne vault of the crossing masks the inside of the tower, originally designed as a lantern. The vault is decorated by bosses bearing the arms of Sir Guy de Brien and with Yorkist badges added after the Battle of Tewkesbury in 1471.

History Chart

*c.*715	Benedictine monastery founded.	1425	Beauchamp chantry constructed.
*c.*1087	Robert Fitzhamon begins building.	1471	Battle of Tewkesbury.
1102	Giraldus and 39 monks move from Cranborne.	1540	Monastery dissolved by King Henry VIII. Abbey purchased from King by townsfolk for £453. Lady Chapel and monastic buildings dismantled.
1121	Consecration of the abbey.		
1178	Monastic buildings destroyed by fire.		
*c.*1310–40	Norman wooden ceiling replaced by vault.	1559	Collapse of spire.
1344	Choir and eastern chapels reconstructed. Choir windows inserted.	1686	West window inserted.
		1875–9	Restoration by Sir George Gilbert Scott.
*c.*1390	Despenser and Fitzhamon chantries constructed.	1971	Queen Elizabeth II distributes the Royal Maundy.

Each day, many visitors come to Tewkesbury Abbey – some to marvel at its history and architecture, some to pray. All, however, speak of the sense of peace and prayer that pervades this glorious church, and how moving it is, each day, to read at Evensong, the prayers left by visitors on our board of intercession. It is through worship and prayer that the true work of the abbey is continued day by day.

I hope that this guide will help you to enjoy your visit here. In it we try to give glimpses of the abbey's long, distinguished and often violent history, and to help you understand its architectural beauty. Despite its size (the second largest in England?), it is very much a parish church, and so we try, too, to give you an idea of its daily work of ministry.

I pray that on your visit, you may experience something of God's presence in this holy place, and that you leave with new inspiration and hope.

Michael Tavinar

VICAR OF TEWKESBURY ABBEY

A Saxon Foundation

Between the Cotswolds and the Malvern Hills, at the confluence of the Rivers Avon and Severn, stands the ancient town of Tewkesbury. Tradition says that it was the site of a Saxon abbey founded around the year AD 715. The abbey's declining fortunes led to its eventually becoming absorbed by Cranborne Abbey in Dorset. All traces of this building have long disappeared.

In 1087 Robert Fitzhamon, a kinsman of William the Conqueror, acquired the Manor of Tewkesbury. Giraldus, Abbot of Cranborne, anxious to extend his dominion, was brought to Tewkesbury and the present abbey was founded with Giraldus as its first Abbot, in the last decade of the 11th century. Robert Fitzhamon died in 1107 from wounds received at the siege of Falaise and his body was buried in the Chapter House of Tewkesbury Abbey.

After Fitzhamon's death, the building work was continued by his son-in-law, Robert Fitzroy, an illegitimate son of King Henry I, who saw the work through to the completion of the Norman phase and the consecration of the church in October 1121. Giraldus had died in 1110 so neither of the founders survived to see the abbey completed. The consecration ceremony was performed by Theulf, the aged Bishop of Worcester, assisted by four other bishops.

Right:
The nave, looking east, is dominated by the great Norman columns. The vault of c.1340 replaced a flat wooden ceiling. The 15 bosses of the central rib tell the story of the life of Our Lord. The bosses of the subsidiary ribs on either side bear angels playing medieval instruments.

Right: ①
The west front showing the recessed Norman arch, 65 feet high (20m) and originally of seven orders. The west window dates from 1686. The north front of Abbey House, originally the Abbot's lodging, is on the right.

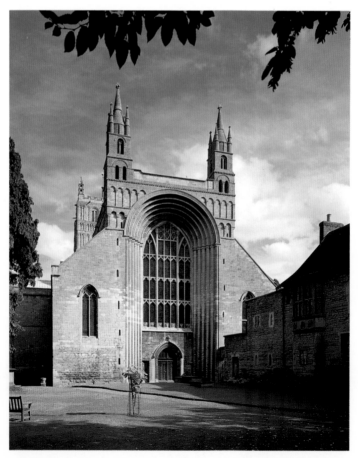

Above: ②
This cross in the north porch dates from the consecration of the abbey in October 1121.

A Great Norman Church

Tewkesbury Abbey bears significant resemblances to its sister church of St Peter's, Gloucester (the present cathedral) in the nave elevation and the ambulatory plan. Twin western towers seem to have been originally planned on the lines of those at Southwell Minster, Nottinghamshire. An indication of this is the thickness of the walls and the solid bays at the west end of the north and south aisles. But plans for this were abandoned. However the superb Norman arch together with its flanking turrets give us what is undoubtedly one of the finest west fronts in England.

The Norman choir and transepts of Tewkesbury were probably the earliest four-storeyed buildings in Europe. The tower, completed in the latter half of the 12th century, is certainly the largest and finest Romanesque tower in England and dominates not only the building but also the town and the surrounding countryside. Its sturdy walls are 46 feet (14m) square and 148 feet (46m) high. The ornate upper stages with the graceful interlaced arches are characteristic of the late Norman period. Only the pinnacles and battlements are not original, having been added in 1600. On all faces of the tower can be seen the inverted 'V' which indicates the original roof line before it was unfortunately lowered in 1614.

Most of the conventual buildings were on the south of the present church. We have become accustomed to seeing the abbey church serene and almost isolated in its churchyards and lawns, and it is difficult to imagine it as it once was, the centre of a huddle of buildings, hemming it in on every side.

On the south side of the nave there are remnants of the 15th-century cloister. The adjacent vaulting indicates the style and the width of the old cloister walk, which was some 80 feet (25m) square. On its eastern side were the slype (a passageway from the monastery into the church) and the Chapter House with a dormitory above. The entrance from the dormitory, now built up, can be seen in the south transept wall.

When we enter the church and stand at the west end of the nave, our view is at once dominated by the 14 enormous columns, each more than 30 feet (9m) high and well over 6 feet (2m) in diameter and surmounted by a Romanesque arch. Above is a rather insignificant triforium with twin openings to each bay. (After the dramatic height of the nave

Below: ⑫
The Lady Chapel. This is the survivor of two Norman apsidal chapels, one in either transept. The mosaic above the altar dates from 1893 and is by Salviati of Venice. The modern sculpture of the Virgin and Child is by Alec Miller.

Left: ⑤
Another misericord;
these were used by the
monks to ease their
standing posture during
lengthy services.

Right: ⑤
A misericord showing
farmyard fowls. The
abbey has a number of
vigorously carved, even
bucolic, scenes.

end of the church once had a magnificent Lady Chapel of which little now remains. It is believed that in the early 16th century this earlier eastern chapel was pulled down. Excavations have revealed foundations 80 feet (25m) long.

The pillars of the choir, originally as tall as those in the nave, were cut down to half their height in the 14th-century reconstruction to provide the basis of the new work.

In the south ambulatory are the tombs of some of the earlier abbots. Among them is the tomb of Abbot Alan who died in 1202. He came to Tewkesbury as Abbot having been Prior of Canterbury and it is his first hand account of the martyrdom of St Thomas Becket, still extant in the British Library, which tells us most of what we know of that tragic event.

columns, perhaps any triforium would appear less than adequate.) The Norman clerestory cannot be fully appreciated owing to the 14th-century vaulting which frequently breaches it. There is no trace of a Norman vault and one must assume that there would have been a wooden ceiling spanning the nave.

About two-thirds of the way along the nave is a shallow step stretching from wall to wall but masked now by three ramps. This is a very significant point in the abbey plan, for it is all that now remains of the screen which divided the people's part of the church from the monastic choir. The impression of the medieval church would have been one of bright, almost garish, colour. The walls were vivid with biblical scenes and the pillars and arches boldly patterned. Of this colour very little now remains. Some may be discerned on the collars of the nave arches nearest the crossing.

On the pillars by the step are the marks of the 'risers' of the two stone staircases which once existed here and which provided access to the top of the screen. From here the gospel would be read to the laity assembled in the nave.

The present Lady Chapel in the south transept is a survivor of a pair, one in either transept. It is a perfect example of a late Norman apsidal chapel. The east

Below: ⑪
The tomb of Abbot
Alan (d.1202). Before his
appointment here as
Abbot, Alan had been
Prior of Christ Church,
Canterbury.

Noble Families

On the death of Robert Fitzroy, the 'Honour of Tewkesbury' reverted to the Crown during the reigns of Henry II and John. It later passed to the great grandson of Robert Fitzroy, Gilbert de Clare, the first of the great family de Clare who were Earls of Gloucester from 1214. The de Clares, the Despensers and the Beauchamps made up the great trio of medieval magnate families who adorned, extended and rebuilt the abbey and have left an enduring mark upon it. Many were buried within its walls; the Despensers clearly regarded it as their particular mausoleum.

The de Clares, Earls of Pembroke and Hertford, had come into the country with William the Conqueror. The first Gilbert de Clare was one of the barons who sealed Magna Carta at Runnymede. His grandson Gilbert II married Joan D'Acre, daughter of King Edward I, and was Lord of Tewkesbury for more than 30 years. His son Gilbert III later inherited the title. Eleanor, his elder sister, married Hugh le Despenser, favourite of King Edward II. On the fall of the king he was captured

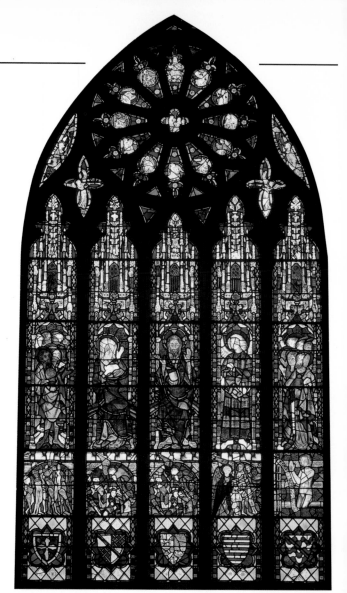

Right: ⑤
Hugh Despenser, as depicted in a window in the choir, was the first husband of Eleanor de Clare who remodelled the choir *c.*1340. He was a favourite of the ill-fated King Edward II and was executed by the rebel barons at Hereford.

Above: ⑧
The east window. At the head, the coronation of the Virgin. The main panels show Christ in majesty, between St Mary the Virgin and St Michael the Archangel. The 12 Apostles are in the outer panels. The donor, Eleanor de Clare, kneels on the right, stripped of all earthly trappings.

by the rebel barons and executed at Hereford. After the death of Hugh, Eleanor and her son (who was also named Hugh) rebuilt and remodelled the whole of the choir and presbytery in the Decorated style, completed the lierne vaulting of the nave and chancel and built the spacious ambulatory with its glorious chevet of chapels.

Hugh and his wife Elizabeth Montacute are buried in the sumptuous tomb on the north side of the high altar. Elizabeth survived Lord Hugh and married Guy de Brien, an early Knight of the Garter, Admiral of the English Fleet which captured Calais, and standard bearer to the English at Crécy. He lies across the aisle from Elizabeth in a tomb obviously modelled on that of Lord Hugh and Elizabeth.

Lord Edward Despenser, nephew of Eleanor and Hugh, built the chantry chapel of the Holy Trinity, an early example of a fan-vaulted building, and which contains a rare, if fragmentary, example of painting in gold leaf on its east wall. Above the roof of the chapel is the unique feature sometimes called the 'kneeling knight'. This is a life-size painted and gilded effigy of Lord Edward in full armour and at prayer. Froissart

Right: (9)
The tomb of Sir Guy de Brien, a patron of the abbey for 40 years until his death in 1390.

Below: (9)
The tomb of Hugh le Despenser (d.1348) and his wife Elizabeth Montacute (d.1359). Their effigies lie beneath a late Decorated canopy, one of the finest in Europe.

described Lord Edward as 'the most honourable, gallant and valiant knight in all England, and much beloved of ladies; the most noble said that no feast was perfect if Sir Despenser was not present'. The male line of the Despensers came to an end with Richard, grandson of Lord Edward and son of Thomas, who supported Richard II and was murdered by Bolingbroke in 1400. Richard's sister Isabella married Richard Beauchamp, Earl of Worcester, and on his death married a distant cousin, also a Richard Beauchamp, the Earl of Warwick. Isabella built the beautiful Beauchamp chantry on the north side of the choir as a memorial to herself and her two Richard Beauchamps.

The Battle of Tewkesbury

Anne, the daughter of Isabella Beauchamp and her second husband, Richard, Earl of Warwick, married Richard Neville ('the Kingmaker') who thus acquired the 'Honour of Tewkesbury', that is, the rights and privileges of the manor.

During the Wars of the Roses, Warwick changed sides more than once and was victorious until he was killed at the Battle of Barnet in 1471 fighting for the Lancastrians, who were, only three weeks later, to suffer a terrible defeat on the field of Tewkesbury.

Margaret of Anjou, queen of the imprisoned Henry VI, had landed with an army at Portland. She set out by forced marches to link up with more Lancastrian supporters in Wales. Arriving at Gloucester to cross the Severn, she found the city fiercely Yorkist in its allegiance. This forced Margaret to turn north along the east bank of the Severn to make for either the ford at Tewkesbury or the bridge at Upton-upon-Severn.

Right:
The inner side of the sacristy door, which is reinforced with strips of metal. These are remains of armour picked up by monks after the Battle of Tewkesbury.

Right: ⑦
The 'kneeling knight', an effigy of Lord Edward Despenser in full armour and at prayer. The gilding is original. Lord of the Manor of Tewkesbury and Knight of the Garter, Lord Edward lived in Tewkesbury from 1358 until his death in 1375. His figure is situated facing the high altar on top of the chantry chapel of the Holy Trinity which he had built.

However, the movements of the Lancastrians were being observed by the Yorkists who were drawn up on the Cotswold escarpment. The Yorkists were commanded by the three royal brothers, King Edward IV, Richard of Gloucester (later to become Richard III) and George, Duke of Clarence, while the Lancastrian commanders were led by the Duke of Somerset, Lord Wenlock and the young Edward of Lancaster, Prince of Wales.

On 3 May 1471, exhausted by their forced marches, the Lancastrians turned to meet their pursuers on the slightly rising ground about a mile south-west of Tewkesbury Abbey. After a hard and bloody struggle the Lancastrians were forced back into the abbey and town. Many of them sought sanctuary in the church where they were pursued by the victorious Yorkists. The story is told that Abbot Strensham was celebrating Mass at the high altar at the time of this invasion of the abbey. Walking the length of the church holding the Blessed Sacrament, he confronted the royal brothers and demanded that the slaughter within the abbey should cease. The King acceded to the Abbot's wishes, but this did not prevent many of the Lancastrians from being dragged out and summarily executed at the cross in the town centre. Edward of Lancaster, the young Prince of Wales, was killed either on the field of battle or shortly afterwards. He is buried in the choir. Many of the flower of the Lancastrian nobility who had fallen in the battle or its aftermath were buried in the north transept of the abbey. Queen Margaret fled to a small religious house at Malvern where she was captured a few days later and sent to the Tower of

Right:
George, Duke of Clarence (d.1474), one of the victorious Yorkist commanders at the Battle of Tewkesbury.

Below: (6)
The Beauchamp or Warwick chantry. The latest and most splendid of the three chantries at Tewkesbury. Erected in 1430 by Isabella Despenser, Countess of Warwick, in memory of herself and her two husbands: (1) Richard Beauchamp, Earl of Worcester and (2) Richard Beauchamp, Earl of Warwick.

London to await ransom by her father. Thus the Lancastrians suffered a terrible defeat at Tewkesbury from which they never really recovered.

One more interesting memorial of the Battle of Tewkesbury still remains. It is said that after the battle the monks walked the site of the fighting picking up the pieces of plate armour which they found littering the ground, and transported them back to the monastery. Here they were hammered flat and used to line the door of the sacristy to make it a kind of primitive strong room door. This is not on general view to the public but is illustrated on the opposite page. The 'Honour of Tewkesbury' was given to George, Duke of Clarence, by his brother King Edward IV. Five years after the Battle of Tewkesbury, Clarence's duchess, Isabella, daughter of Warwick the King-maker, died in childbirth. Clarence himself, 'false, fleeting, perjured Clarence' according to Shakespeare, was murdered in the Tower of London. The remains of Clarence and his wife lie in a vault behind the high altar. Thus ended the connection with Tewkesbury of the de Clares, the Despensers, the Beauchamps and the Clarences.

Turbulent Times

With the dissolution of the monasteries in the years 1535–40, Henry VIII, effected a social revolution which marked the end of the Middle Ages in England. His national church, no longer under papal rule, finally acknowledged the superiority of the laity over the clergy, and enabled the Church's vast wealth and land to be divided among the rising new middle class.

It is true that in general the monasteries had not been good managers of their huge wealth, but the way in which monastic lands and possessions were disposed of was little short of criminal. The

Right:
The Abbot's gateway, a late medieval entrance, restored in 1849 by Medland, and in 1991 by the Landmark Trust.

Below: ⑤
The choir vault. A marvellous 14th-century stellar vault, painted and gilded, and later decorated with the Yorkist badges of the sun in splendour.

monasteries had by this time ceased to be an intellectual force. The proportion of their income used for almsgiving and other good works had by then become very small. The new interest in biblical and classical learning was not pursued to any great extent in the monasteries, and life within their walls was no longer ascetic or devoted to hard manual labour. Manuscripts recording episcopal visitations of monasteries and religious houses of this period provide a great deal of evidence of the declining influence and indeed, in some cases, scandalous conduct of the monasteries. There is no evidence, however, that there was corruption at Tewkesbury.

For over 400 years since its foundation, the great abbey of Tewkesbury, under the patronage of the greatest families in the land, had been amassing wealth until it had become one of the richest in England. In the year before its dissolution its revenues were over £300,000 in today's money. The abbey was finally surrendered to the King's commissioners on 9 January 1540. Its possessions, listed on 74 sheets of parchment, were seized by the Crown, and silver vessels and plate, over 100 lbs in weight, went into the royal coffers. The commissioners ordered the dismantling and destruction of the great Lady Chapel at the east end of the church, and the monastic buildings.

The monks of the abbey were granted small pensions, and the last Abbot, John Wakeman acquired Forthampton Court, a fine Tudor house some two miles or so north of Tewkesbury. The King also created him the first Bishop of the new see of Gloucester. The so-called Wakeman cenotaph is his memorial here, a grisly *memento mori*, in the fashion of a hundred years earlier. It depicts the cadaver of a monk covered in vermin, snake, frog, rat and snail, all feasting on the corpse. This effigy should be at ground level, and another in full ecclesiastical vestments should occupy the upper level. This is a well-known form of medieval ecclesiastical monument and is meant to illustrate the transitoriness of earthly things. *'Sic transit gloria Mundi'*. John Wakeman is not buried here, nor is he interred at Gloucester. He rests beside the altar in Forthampton Church.

Below: ⑩
The eastern ambulatory, with, on the right, the 19th-century window donated by the Revd Charles Grove. This wall dates from the mid-16th century. The medieval Lady Chapel which extended the church by some 80 feet (25m) eastward lay beyond it. In the background can be seen the so-called Wakeman cenotaph.

A Parish Church

After the suppression of the monastery, the good people of Tewkesbury, who had been accustomed to using the western part of the nave for worship, approached the King through his commissioners and petitioned him for permission to purchase the whole church for use as their parish church. The King charged them the value of the metal in the bells and the lead on the roof, a considerable sum for them to find, no less than £453. To their eternal credit the townsfolk raised this sum in two years, and thanks to their generosity and foresight the abbey still stands for us and for our descendants to use and enjoy.

The Crown seized all the abbey lands and endowments. The manor it already held. King James I sold the manor to the Corporation of Tewkesbury for £2,454 in 1609, retaining the right to appoint the Vicar. This right is still exercised by the Crown through the Lord Chancellor.

In the choir is the renowned 'Milton' organ, regarded by organists as a national treasure. The earliest parts are by Thomas Dallam, a noted Jacobean organ builder who constructed the instrument originally for Magdalen College, Oxford. During the Commonwealth it was removed to the chapel of Hampton Court Palace where, one may assume, it was played by the aspiring poet John Milton, then Latin Secretary to Oliver Cromwell. Milton, before his blindness, was a keen musician and able organist. The organ

Right:
The abbey from the north-east. The magnificent Norman tower dominates and dwarfs the building. Originally, the Lady Chapel would have existed here, joining the main building at the wall below the turrets in the left foreground.

Right: ①
A detail from the west window depicting The Last Supper. The window is one of the many gifts to the abbey from the Revd Charles Grove. Made by Hardman of Birmingham in 1888, it is divided into nine sections, each of which represents a scene from the gospel stories.

later went back to Magdalen College, to be brought to Tewkesbury in 1737.

In the north transept is another organ, regarded as a supreme example of Victorian organ building and presented to the abbey in 1887 by the Revd. Charles Grove, a great benefactor of the abbey. He was never an incumbent of Tewkesbury, but was a curate of Newland in the Forest of Dean. His many other generous gifts to the abbey include the lectern, the glass in the west window, the windows of the nave and the east window in the ambulatory. The face of the publican in this last window is said to be a portrait of the donor.

Tewkesbury Abbey has no less than 17 bells, 13 of them hung for ringing and 4 clock bells which are struck to mark the quarter hours. The tenor bell weighs over 27 cwt.

Right: ⑤
The 'Milton' organ. This beautiful instrument dating from the 17th century stands in the south choir. Beyond is the south transept and in the foreground, the choir stalls.

The Church Today and Tomorrow

'For Claire, suffering from cancer'
'For Tim and Mary, for their marriage'
'For my dear Dad who died last week'

Prayers such as these appear each day on the intercession board in the Lady Chapel of the abbey. Who wrote them? Why did they leave them? Many people who visit the abbey glimpse God in its beauty and feel drawn to pray and meet God afresh.

Its ancient walls are soaked in prayer. For over 400 years these walls heard the eightfold office of the Benedictine monks and, since the Reformation, the work of prayer has continued, through the liturgy, through the prayers of parishioners, and now, even more, through the prayers of its many visitors.

Worship is at the heart of the abbey's witness and mission. Although firmly rooted in the Catholic tradition of the Church of England, we seek to be broad and open in our interpretation of this. Thus, in the abbey you can find quiet weekday Eucharists, a Healing Eucharist with modern choruses, the Pram Service, a Family Service, with the children

Below:
The Eucharist or Mass is celebrated Sunday by Sunday at the high altar.

making their important contribution, the full splendour and drama of the High Mass, with its ceremonial and music, and daily Choral Evensong. Such variety reflects, we hope, the myriad ways in which God comes to us, and helps us to respond to each other with understanding of differences in worship and approach.

The abbey is probably the second largest parish church in England and we value our pastoral role, and have our fair share of baptisms, weddings and funerals, with all the contacts that these give. The range of parish activities is large and we value also our links with uniformed organizations, the Guides, Brownies and the Boys' Brigade, who worship with us

Right: ③
Baptism. The font is traditionally and symbolically placed near the entrance to the church. By being baptized we enter the life of Christian discipleship. Next to the font stands the great Easter candle, symbolizing our transition from darkness to light; from a world of sin and death to a world of God's love and enduring life.

Below left: ④
Reading from the lectern in the nave.

Below:
The Easter garden. Each Easter we build, in the Chapel of the Holy Cross, a life-size representation of the empty tomb and Calvary with its empty crosses.

regularly. It is also as a parish church that we work and develop our life with other Christians in Tewkesbury and the district. New areas of work seem to be opening up for us with emphasis on Christian teaching and nurture, preparation for baptism and marriage, and other ways in which we can be more effective in proclaiming the Gospel of Christ.

But Tewkesbury Abbey has a role larger than that of just a parish church to the town's inhabitants. Besides our many thousands of visitors, a great number of people pass through its doors to attend concerts, recitals, plays and special services. In this way the people of Tewkesbury use their special resources to proclaim God through music, drama, art and architecture. Our hope is that those who come to the abbey to see this incomparable example of medieval architecture, will find their visit not just of historical value but also of spiritual significance on their Christian pilgrimage.

If you came this way,
Taking any route, starting from anywhere,
At any time or at any season,
It would always be the same;
*   you would have to put off*
Sense and notion, You are not here to verify,
Instruct yourself, or inform curiosity,
Or carry report, You are here to kneel
Where prayer has been valid.

T.S. ELIOT — FOUR QUARTETS

Right:
Recessional: the Eucharist or Mass is ended and the choir and clergy move through the congregation. 'Go in peace to love and serve the Lord.'